The Growth of Love by Robert Seymour Bridges

Robert Bridges was born in Walmer, Kent on the 23rd of October 1844. He went to study medicine intending to practice until the age of forty and then retire to write poetry.

Lung disease forced him to retire in 1882, and from that point on he devoted himself to writing and literary research. However, Bridges' literary work started long before his retirement, his first collection of poems having been published in 1873.

He was appointed Poet Laureate in 1913 by George V, the only medical graduate to have held the office.

He died in Oxford on the 21st of April 1930.

Index of Contents

THE GROWTH OF LOVE

I

They that in play can do the thing they would,
Having an instinct throned in reason's place,
—And every perfect action hath the grace
Of indolence or thoughtless hardihood—
These are the best: yet be there workmen good
Who lose in earnestness control of face,
Or reckon means, and rapt in effort base
Reach to their end by steps well understood.

Me whom thou sawest of late strive with the pains
Of one who spends his strength to rule his nerve,
—Even as a painter breathlessly who strains
His scarcely moving hand lest it should swerve—
Behold me, now that I have cast my chains,
Master of the art which for thy sake I serve.

II

For thou art mine: and now I am ashamed

To have usèd means to win so pure acquist,
And of my trembling fear that might have misst
Thro' very care the gold at which I aim'd;
And am as happy but to hear thee named,
As are those gentle souls by angels kisst
In pictures seen leaving their marble cist
To go before the throne of grace unblamed.

Nor surer am I water hath the skill
To quench my thirst, or that my strength is freed
In delicate ordination as I will,
Than that to be myself is all I need
For thee to be most mine: so I stand still,
And save to taste my joy no more take heed.

III

The whole world now is but the minister
Of thee to me: I see no other scheme
But universal love, from timeless dream
Waking to thee his joy's interpreter.
I walk around and in the fields confer
Of love at large with tree and flower and stream,
And list the lark descant upon my theme,
Heaven's musical accepted worshipper.

Thy smile outfaceth ill: and that old feud
'Twixt things and me is quash'd in our new truce;
And nature now dearly with thee endued
No more in shame ponders her old excuse,
But quite forgets her frowns and antics rude,
So kindly hath she grown to her new use.

IV

The very names of things belov'd are dear,
And sounds will gather beauty from their sense,
As many a face thro' love's long residence
Groweth to fair instead of plain and sere:
But when I say thy name it hath no peer,
And I suppose fortune determined thence
Her dower, that such beauty's excellence
Should have a perfect title for the ear.

Thus may I think the adopting Muses chose
Their sons by name, knowing none would be heard

Or writ so oft in all the world as those,—
Dan Chaucer, mighty Shakespeare, then for third
The classic Milton, and to us arose
Shelley with liquid music in the word.

V

The poets were good teachers, for they taught
Earth had this joy; but that 'twould ever be
That fortune should be perfected in me,
My heart of hope dared not engage the thought.
So I stood low, and now but to be caught
By any self-styled lords of the age with thee
Vexes my modesty, lest they should see
I hold them owls and peacocks, things of nought.

And when we sit alone, and as I please
I taste thy love's full smile, and can enstate
The pleasure of my kingly heart at ease,
My thought swims like a ship, that with the weight
Of her rich burden sleeps on the infinite seas
Becalm'd, and cannot stir her golden freight.

VI

While yet we wait for spring, and from the dry
And blackening east that so embitters March,
Well-housed must watch grey fields and meadows parch,
And driven dust and withering snowflake fly:
Already in glimpses of the tarnish'd sky
The sun is warm and beckons to the larch,
And where the covert hazels interarch
Their tassell'd twigs, fair beds of primrose lie.

Beneath the crisp and wintry carpet hid
A million buds but stay their blossoming;
And trustful birds have built their nests amid
The shuddering boughs, and only wait to sing
Till one soft shower from the south shall bid,
And hither tempt the pilgrim steps of spring.

VII

In thee my spring of life hath bid the while
A rose unfold beyond the summer's best,

The mystery of joy made manifest
In love's self-answering and awakening smile,
Whereby the lips in wonder reconcile
Passion with peace, and show desire at rest,—
A grace of silence by the Greek unguesst,
That bloom'd to immortalize the Tuscan style:

When first the angel-song that faith hath ken'd
Fancy pourtray'd, above recorded oath
Of Israel's God, or light of poem pen'd;
The very countenance of plighted troth
'Twixt heaven and earth, where in one moment blend
The hope of one and happiness of both.

VIII

For beauty being the best of all we know
Sums up the unsearchable and secret aims
Of nature, and on joys whose earthly names
Were never told can form and sense bestow;
And man hath sped his instinct to outgo
The step of science; and against her shames
Imagination stakes out heavenly claims,
Building a tower above the head of woe.

Nor is there fairer work for beauty found
Than that she win in nature her release
From all the woes that in the world abound:
Nay with his sorrow may his love increase,
If from man's greater need beauty redound,
And claim his tears for homage of his peace.

IX

Thus to thy beauty doth my fond heart look,
That late dismay'd her faithless faith forbore;
And wins again her love lost in the lore
Of schools and script of many a learned book:
For thou what ruthless death untimely took
Shalt now in better brotherhood restore,
And save my batter'd ship that far from shore
High on the dismal deep in tempest shook.

So in despite of sorrow lately learn'd
I still hold true to truth since thou art true,
Nor wail the woe which thou to joy hast turn'd:

Nor come the heavenly sun and bathing blue
To my life's need more splendid and unearn'd
Than hath thy gift outmatch'd desire and due.

X

Winter was not unkind because uncouth;
His prison'd time made me a closer guest,
And gave thy graciousness a warmer zest,
Biting all else with keen and angry tooth:
And bravelier the triumphant blood of youth
Mantling thy cheek its happy home possest,
And sterner sport by day put strength to test,
And custom's feast at night gave tongue to truth.

Or say hath flaunting summer a device
To match our midnight revelry, that rang
With steel and flame along the snow-girt ice?
Or when we hark't to nightingales that sang
On dewy eves in spring, did they entice
To gentler love than winter's icy fang?

XI

There's many a would-be poet at this hour,
Rhymes of a love that he hath never woo'd,
And o'er his lamplit desk in solitude
Deems that he sitteth in the Muses' bower:
And some the flames of earthly love devour,
Who have taken no kiss of Nature, nor renew'd
In the world's wilderness with heavenly food
The sickly body of their perishing power.

So none of all our company, I boast,
But now would mock my penning, coud they see
How down the right it maps a jagged coast;
Seeing they hold the manlier praise to be
Strong hand and will, and the heart best when most
'Tis sober, simple, true, and fancy-free.

XII

How coud I quarrel or blame you, most dear,
Who all thy virtues gavest and kept back none;
Kindness and gentleness, truth without peer,

And beauty that my fancy fed upon?
Now not my life's contrition for my fault
Can blot that day, nor work me recompence,
Tho' I might worthily thy worth exalt,
Making thee long amends for short offence.

For surely nowhere, love, if not in thee
Are grace and truth and beauty to be found;
And all my praise of these can only be
A praise of thee, howe'er by thee disown'd:
While still thou must be mine tho' far removed,
And I for one offence no more beloved.

XIII

Now since to me altho' by thee refused
The world is left, I shall find pleasure still;
The art that most I have loved but little used
Will yield a world of fancies at my will:
And tho' where'er thou goest it is from me,
I where I go thee in my heart must bear;
And what thou wert that wilt thou ever be,
My choice, my best, my loved, and only fair.

Farewell, yet think not such farewell a change
From tenderness, tho' once to meet or part
But on short absence so coud sense derange
That tears have graced the greeting of my heart;
They were proud drops and had my leave to fall,
Not on thy pity for my pain to call.

XIV

When sometimes in an ancient house where state
From noble ancestry is handed on,
We see but desolation thro' the gate,
And richest heirlooms all to ruin gone;
Because maybe some fancied shame or fear,
Bred of disease or melancholy fate,
Hath driven the owner from his rightful sphere
To wander nameless save to pity or hate:

What is the wreck of all he hath in fief,
When he that hath is wrecking? nought is fine
Unto the sick, nor doth it burden grief
That the house perish when the soul doth pine.

Thus I my state despise, slain by a sting
So slight 'twould not have hurt a meaner thing.

XV

Who builds a ship must first lay down the keel
Of health, whereto the ribs of mirth are wed:
And knit, with beams and knees of strength, a bed
For decks of purity, her floor and ceil.
Upon her masts, Adventure, Pride, and Zeal,
To fortune's wind the sails of purpose spread:
And at the prow make figured maidenhead
O'erride the seas and answer to the wheel.

And let him deep in memory's hold have stor'd
Water of Helicon: and let him fit
The needle that doth true with heaven accord:
Then bid her crew, love, diligence and wit
With justice, courage, temperance come aboard,
And at her helm the master reason sit.

XVI

This world is unto God a work of art,
Of which the unaccomplish'd heavenly plan
Is hid in life within the creature's heart,
And for perfection looketh unto man.
Ah me! those thousand ages: with what slow
Pains and persistence were his idols made,
Destroy'd and made, ere ever he coud know
The mighty mother must be so obey'd.

For lack of knowledge and thro' little skill
His childish mimicry outwent his aim;
His effort shaped the genius of his will;
Till thro' distinction and revolt he came,
True to his simple terms of good and ill,
Seeking the face of Beauty without blame.

XVII

Say who be these light-bearded, sunburnt faces
In negligent and travel-stain'd array,
That in the city of Dante come to-day,
Haughtily visiting her holy places?

O these be noble men that hide their graces,
True England's blood, her ancient glory's stay,
By tales of fame diverted on their way
Home from the rule of oriental races.

Life-trifling lions these, of gentle eyes
And motion delicate, but swift to fire
For honour, passionate where duty lies,
Most loved and loving: and they quickly tire
Of Florence, that she one day more denies
The embrace of wife and son, of sister or sire.

XVIII

Where San Miniato's convent from the sun
At forenoon overlooks the city of flowers
I sat, and gazing on her domes and towers
Call'd up her famous children one by one:
And three who all the rest had far outdone,
Mild Giotto first, who stole the morning hours,
I saw, and god-like Buonarroti's powers,
And Dante, gravest poet, her much-wrong'd son.

Is all this glory, I said, another's praise?
Are these heroic triumphs things of old,
And do I dead upon the living gaze?
Or rather doth the mind, that can behold
The wondrous beauty of the works and days,
Create the image that her thoughts enfold?

XIX

Rejoice, ye dead, where'er your spirits dwell,
Rejoice that yet on earth your fame is bright;
And that your names, remember'd day and night,
Live on the lips of those that love you well.
'Tis ye that conquer'd have the powers of hell,
Each with the special grace of your delight:
Ye are the world's creators, and thro' might
Of everlasting love ye did excel.

Now ye are starry names, above the storm
And war of Time and nature's endless wrong
Ye flit, in pictured truth and peaceful form,
Wing'd with bright music and melodious song,—
The flaming flowers of heaven, making May-dance

In dear Imagination's rich pleasance.

THE world still goeth about to shew and hide,
Befool'd of all opinion, fond of fame:
But he that can do well taketh no pride,
And see'th his error, undisturb'd by shame:
So poor's the best that longest life can do,
The most so little, diligently done;
So mighty is the beauty that doth woo,
So vast the joy that love from love hath won.

God's love to win is easy, for He loveth
Desire's fair attitude, nor strictly weighs
The broken thing, but all alike approveth
Which love hath aim'd at Him: that is heaven's praise:
And if we look for any praise on earth,
'Tis in man's love: all else is nothing worth.

O flesh and blood, comrade to tragic pain
And clownish merriment; whose sense could wake
Sermons in stones, and count death but an ache,
All things as vanity, yet nothing vain:
The world, set in thy heart, thy passionate strain
Reveal'd anew; but thou for man didst make
Nature twice natural, only to shake
Her kingdom with the creatures of thy brain.

Lo, Shakespeare, since thy time nature is loth
To yield to art her fair supremacy;
In conquering one thou hast so enrichèd both.
What shall I say? for God—whose wise decree
Confirmeth all He did by all He doth—
Doubled His whole creation making thee.

I would be a bird, and straight on wings I arise,
And carry purpose up to the ends of the air:
In calm and storm my sails I feather, and where
By freezing cliffs the unransom'd wreckage lies:
Or, strutting on hot meridian banks, surprise

The silence: over plains in the moonlight bare
I chase my shadow, and perch where no bird dare
In treetops torn by fiercest winds of the skies.

Poor simple birds, foolish birds! then I cry,
Ye pretty pictures of delight, unstir'd
By the only joy of knowing that ye fly;
Ye are nót what ye are, but rather, sum'd in a word,
The alphabet of a god's idea, and I
Who master it, I am the only bird.

XXIII

O weary pilgrims, chanting of your woe,
That turn your eyes to all the peaks that shine,
Hailing in each the citadel divine
The which ye thought to have enter'd long ago;
Until at length your feeble steps and slow
Falter upon the threshold of the shrine,
And your hearts overburden'd doubt in fine
Whether it be Jerusalem or no:

Dishearten'd pilgrims, I am one of you;
For, having worshipp'd many a barren face,
I scarce now greet the goal I journey'd to:
I stand a pagan in the holy place;
Beneath the lamp of truth I am found untrue,
And question with the God that I embrace.

XXIV

Spring hath her own bright days of calm and peace;
Her melting air, at every breath we draw,
Floods heart with love to praise God's gracious law:
But suddenly—so short is pleasure's lease—
The cold returns, the buds from growing cease,
And nature's conquer'd face is full of awe;
As now the trait'rous north with icy flaw
Freezes the dew upon the sick lamb's fleece,

And 'neath the mock sun searching everywhere
Rattles the crispèd leaves with shivering din:
So that the birds are silent with despair
Within the thickets; nor their armour thin
Will gaudy flies adventure in the air,
Nor any lizard sun his spotted skin.

XXV

Nothing is joy without thee: I can find
No rapture in the first relays of spring,
In songs of birds, in young buds opening,
Nothing inspiriting and nothing kind;
For lack of thee, who once wert throned behind
All beauty, like a strength where graces cling, —
The jewel and heart of light, which everything
Wrestled in rivalry to hold enshrined.

Ah! since thou'rt fled, and I in each fair sight
The sweet occasion of my joy deplore,
Where shall I seek thee best, or whom invite
Within thy sacred temples and adore?
Who shall fill thought and truth with old delight,
And lead my soul in life as heretofore?

XXVI

The work is done, and from the fingers fall
The bloodwarm tools that brought the labour thro':
The tasking eye that overrunneth all
Rests, and affirms there is no more to do.
Now the third joy of making, the sweet flower
Of blessed work, bloometh in godlike spirit;
Which whoso plucketh holdeth for an hour
The shrivelling vanity of mortal merit.

And thou, my perfect work, thou'rt of to-day;
To-morrow a poor and alien thing wilt be,
True only should the swift life stand at stay:
Therefore farewell, nor look to bide with me.
Go find thy friends, if there be one to love thee:
Casting thee forth, my child, I rise above thee.

XXVII

The fabled sea-snake, old Leviathan,
Or else what grisly beast of scaly chine
That champ'd the ocean-wrack and swash'd the brine,
Before the new and milder days of man,
Had never rib nor bray nor swindging fan
Like his iron swimmer of the Clyde or Tyne,

Late-born of golden seed to breed a line
Of offspring swifter and more huge of plan.

Straight is her going, for upon the sun
When once she hath look'd, her path and place are plain;
With tireless speed she smiteth one by one
The shuddering seas and foams along the main;
And her eased breath, when her wild race is run,
Roars thro' her nostrils like a hurricane.

XXVIII

A thousand times hath in my heart's behoof
My tongue been set his passion to impart;
A thousand times hath my too coward heart
My mouth reclosed and fix'd it to the roof;
Then with such cunning hath it held aloof,
A thousand times kept silence with such art
That words coud do no more: yet on thy part
Hath silence given a thousand times reproof.

I should be bolder, seeing I commend
Love, that my dilatory purpose primes,
But fear lest with my fears my hope should end:
Nay, I would truth deny and burn my rhymes,
Renew my sorrows rather than offend,
A thousand times, and yet a thousand times.

XXIX

I travel to thee with the sun's first rays,
That lift the dark west and unwrap the night;
I dwell beside thee when he walks the height,
And fondly toward thee at his setting gaze.
I wait upon thy coming, but always—
Dancing to meet my thoughts if they invite—
Thou hast outrun their longing with delight,
And in my solitude dost mock my praise.

Now doth my drop of time transcend the whole:
I see no fame in Khufu's pyramid,
No history where loveless Nile doth roll.
—This is eternal life, which doth forbid
Mortal detraction to the exalted soul,
And from her inward eye all fate hath hid.

XXX

My lady pleases me and I please her;
This know we both, and I besides know well
Wherefore I love her, and I love to tell
My love, as all my loving songs aver.
But what on her part could the passion stir,
Tho' 'tis more difficult for love to spell,
Yet can I dare divine how this befel,
Nor will her lips deny it if I err.

She loves me first because I love her, then
Loves me for knowing why she should be loved.
And that I love to praise her, loves again.
So from her beauty both our loves are moved,
And by her beauty are sustain'd; nor when
The earth falls from the sun is this disproved.

XXXI

In all things beautiful, I cannot see
Her sit or stand, but love is stir'd anew:
'Tis joy to watch the folds fall as they do,
And all that comes is past expectancy.
If she be silent, silence let it be;
He who would bid her speak might sit and sue
The deep-brow'd Phidian Jove to be untrue
To his two thousand years' solemnity.

Ah, but her launchèd passion, when she sings,
Wins on the hearing like a shapen prow
Borne by the mastery of its urgent wings:
Or if she deign her wisdom, she doth show
She hath the intelligence of heavenly things,
Unsullied by man's mortal overthrow.

XXXII

Thus to be humbled: 'tis that ranging pride
No refuge hath; that in his castle strong
Brave reason sits beleaguer'd, who so long
Kept field, but now must starve where he doth hide;
That industry, who once the foe defied,
Lies slaughter'd in the trenches; that the throng
Of idle fancies pipe their foolish song,

Where late the puissant captains fought and died.

Thus to be humbled: 'tis to be undone;
A forest fell'd; a city razed to ground;
A cloak unsewn, unwoven and unspun
Till not a thread remains that can be wound.
And yet, O lover, thee, the ruin'd one,
Love who hath humbled thus hath also crown'd.

XXXIII

I care not if I live, tho' life and breath
Have never been to me so dear and sweet.
I care not if I die, for I coud meet—
Being so happy—happily my death.
I care not if I love; to-day she saith
She loveth, and love's history is complete.
Nor care I if she love me; at her feet
My spirit bows entranced and worshippeth.

I have no care for what was most my care,
But all around me see fresh beauty born,
And common sights grown lovelier than they were:
I dream of love, and in the light of morn
Tremble, beholding all things very fair
And strong with strength that puts my strength to scorn.

XXXIV

O my goddess divine sometimes I say:—
Now let this word for ever and all suffice;
Thou art insatiable, and yet not twice
Can even thy lover give his soul away:
And for my acts, that at thy feet I lay;
For never any other, by device
Of wisdom, love or beauty, could entice
My homage to the measure of this day.

I have no more to give thee: lo, I have sold
My life, have emptied out my heart, and spent
Whate'er I had; till like a beggar, bold
With nought to lose, I laugh and am content.
A beggar kisses thee; nay, love, behold,
I fear not: thou too art in beggarment.

XXXV

All earthly beauty hath one cause and proof,
To lead the pilgrim soul to beauty above:
Yet lieth the greater bliss so far aloof,
That few there be are wean'd from earthly love.
Joy's ladder it is, reaching from home to home,
The best of all the work that all was good;
Whereof 'twas writ the angels aye upclomb,
Down sped, and at the top the Lord God stood.

But I my time abuse, my eyes by day
Center'd on thee, by night my heart on fire—
Letting my number'd moments run away—
Nor e'en 'twixt night and day to heaven aspire:
So true it is that what the eye seeth not
But slow is loved, and loved is soon forgot.

XXXVI

O my life's mischief, once my love's delight,
That drew'st a mortgage on my heart's estate,
Whose baneful clause is never out of date,
Nor can avenging time restore my right:
Whom first to lose sounded that note of spite,
Whereto my doleful days were tuned by fate:
That art the well-loved cause of all my hate,
The sun whose wandering makes my hopeless night:

Thou being in all my lacking all I lack,
It is thy goodness turns my grace to crime,
Thy fleetness from my goal which holds me back;
Wherefore my feet go out of step with time,
My very grasp of life is old and slack,
And even my passion falters in my rhyme.

XXXVII

At times with hurried hoofs and scattering dust
I race by field or highway, and my horse
Spare not, but urge direct in headlong course
Unto some fair far hill that gain I must:
But near arrived the vision soon mistrust,
Rein in, and stand as one who sees the source
Of strong illusion, shaming thought to force
From off his mind the soil of passion's gust.

My brow I bare then, and with slacken'd speed
Can view the country pleasant on all sides,
And to kind salutation give good heed:
I ride as one who for his pleasure rides,
And stroke the neck of my delighted steed,
And seek what cheer the village inn provides.

XXXVIII

An idle June day on the sunny Thames,
Floating or rowing as our fancy led,
Now in the high beams basking as we sped,
Now in green shade gliding by mirror'd stems;
By lock and weir and isle, and many a spot
Of memoried pleasure, glad with strength and skill,
Friendship, good wine, and mirth, that serve not ill
The heavenly Muse, tho' she requite them not:

I would have life—thou saidst—all as this day,
Simple enjoyment calm in its excess,
With not a grief to cloud, and not a ray
Of passion overhot my peace to oppress;
With no ambition to reproach delay,
Nor rapture to disturb its happiness.

XXXIX

A man that sees by chance his picture, made
As once a child he was, handling some toy,
Will gaze to find his spirit within the boy,
Yet hath no secret with the soul pourtray'd:
He cannot think the simple thought which play'd
Upon those features then so frank and coy;
'Tis his, yet oh! not his: and o'er the joy
His fatherly pity bends in tears dismay'd.

Proud of his prime maybe he stand at best,
And lightly wear his strength, or aim it high,
In knowledge, skill and courage self-possest:—
Yet in the pictured face a charm doth lie,
The one thing lost more worth than all the rest,
Which seeing, he fears to say This child was I.

XL

Tears of love, tears of joy and tears of care,
Comforting tears that fell uncomforted,
Tears o'er the new-born, tears beside the dead,
Tears of hope, pride and pity, trust and prayer,
Tears of contrition; all tears whatsoe'er
Of tenderness or kindness had she shed
Who here is pictured, ere upon her head
The fine gold might be turn'd to silver there.

The smile that charm'd the father hath given place
Unto the furrow'd care wrought by the son;
But virtue hath transform'd all change to grace:
So that I praise the artist, who hath done
A portrait, for my worship, of the face
Won by the heart my father's heart that won.

XLI

If I coud but forget and not recall
So well my time of pleasure and of play,
When ancient nature was all new and gay,
Light as the fashion that doth last enthrall,—
Ah mighty nature, when my heart was small,
Nor dream'd what fearful searchings underlay
The flowers and leafy ecstasy of May,
The breathing summer sloth, the scented fall:

Coud I forget, then were the fight not hard,
Press'd in the mêlée of accursed things,
Having such help in love and such reward:
But that 'tis I who once—'tis this that stings—
Once dwelt within the gate that angels guard,
Where yet I'd be had I but heavenly wings.

XLII

When I see childhood on the threshold seize
The prize of life from age and likelihood,
I mourn time's change that will not be withstood,
Thinking how Christ said Be like one of these.
For in the forest among many trees
Scarce one in all is found that hath made good
The virgin pattern of its slender wood,
That courtesied in joy to every breeze;

But scath'd, but knotted trunks that raise on high
Their arms in stiff contortion, strain'd and bare;
Whose patriarchal crowns in sorrow sigh.
So, little children, ye—nay nay, ye ne'er
From me shall learn how sure the change and nigh,
When ye shall share our strength and mourn to share.

XLIII

When parch'd with thirst, astray on sultry sand
The traveller faints, upon his closing ear
Steals a fantastic music: he may hear
The babbling fountain of his native land.
Before his eyes the vision seems to stand,
Where at its terraced brink the maids appear,
Who fill their deep urns at its waters clear,
And not refuse the help of lover's hand.

O cruel jest—he cries, as some one flings
The sparkling drops in sport or shew of ire—
O shameless, O contempt of holy things.
But never of their wanton play they tire,
As not athirst they sit beside the springs,
While he must quench in death his lost desire.

XLIV

The image of thy love, rising on dark
And desperate days over my sullen sea,
Wakens again fresh hope and peace in me,
Gleaming above upon my groaning bark.
Whate'er my sorrow be, I then may hark
A loving voice: whate'er my terror be,
This heavenly comfort still I win from thee,
To shine my lodestar that wert once my mark.

Prodigal nature makes us but to taste
One perfect joy, which given she niggard grows;
And lest her precious gift should run to waste,
Adds to its loss a thousand lesser woes:
So to the memory of the gift that graced
Her hand, her graceless hand more grace bestows.

XLV

In this neglected, ruin'd edifice
Of works unperfected and broken schemes,
Where is the promise of my early dreams,
The smile of beauty and the pearl of price?
No charm is left now that could once entice
Wind-wavering fortune from her golden streams,
And full in flight decrepit purpose seems,
Trailing the banner of his old device.

Within the house a frore and numbing air
Has chill'd endeavour: sickly memories reign
In every room, and ghosts are on the stair:
And hope behind the dusty window-pane
Watches the days go by, and bow'd with care
Forecasts her last reproach and mortal stain.

XLVI

Once I would say, before thy vision came,
My joy, my life, my love, and with some kind
Of knowledge speak, and think I knew my mind
Of heaven and hope, and each word hit its aim.
Whate'er their sounds be, now all mean the same,
Denoting each the fair that none can find;
Or if I say them, 'tis as one long blind
Forgets the sights that he was used to name.

Now if men speak of love, 'tis not my love;
Nor are their hopes nor joys mine, nor their life
Of praise the life that I think honour of:
Nay tho' they turn from house and child and wife
And self, and in the thought of heaven above
Hold, as do I, all mortal things at strife.

XLVII

Since then 'tis only pity looking back,
Fear looking forward, and the busy mind
Will in one woeful moment more upwind
Than lifelong years unroll of bitter or black;
What is man's privilege, his hoarding knack
Of memory with foreboding so combined,
Whereby he comes to dream he hath of kind
The perpetuity which all things lack?

Which but to hope is doubtful joy, to have

Being a continuance of what, alas,
We mourn, and scarcely bear with to the grave;
Or something so unknown that it o'erpass
The thought of comfort, and the sense that gave
Cannot consider it thro' any glass.

XLVIII

Come gentle sleep, I woo thee: come and take
Not now the child into thine arms, from fright
Composed by drowsy tune and shaded light,
Whom ignorant of thee thou didst nurse and make;
Nor now the boy, who scorn'd thee for the sake
Of growing knowledge or mysterious night,
Tho' with fatigue thou didst his limbs invite,
And heavily weigh the eyes that would not wake;

No, nor the man severe, who from his best
Failing, alert fled to thee, that his breath,
Blood, force and fire should come at morn redrest;
But me, from whom thy comfort tarrieth,
For all my wakeful prayer sent without rest
To thee, O shew and shadow of my death.

XLIX

The spirit's eager sense for sad or gay
Filleth with what he will our vessel full:
Be joy his bent, he waiteth not joy's day
But like a child at any toy will pull:
If sorrow, he will weep for fancy's sake,
And spoil heaven's plenty with forbidden care.
What fortune most denies we slave to take;
Nor can fate load us more than we can bear.

Since pleasure with the having disappeareth,
He who hath least in hand hath most at heart,
While he keep hope: as he who alway feareth
A grief that never comes hath yet the smart;
And heavier far is our self-wrought distress,
For when God sendeth sorrow, it doth bless.

L

The world comes not to an end: her city-hives

Swarm with the tokens of a changeless trade,
With rolling wheel, driver and flagging jade,
Rich men and beggars, children, priests and wives.
New homes on old are set, as lives on lives;
Invention with invention overlaid:
But still or tool or toy or book or blade
Shaped for the hand, that holds and toils and strives.

The men to-day toil as their fathers taught,
With little better'd means; for works depend
On works and overlap, and thought on thought:
And thro' all change the smiles of hope amend
The weariest face, the same love changed in nought:
In this thing too the world comes not to an end.

LI

O my uncared-for songs, what are ye worth,
That in my secret book with so much care
I write you, this one here and that one there,
Marking the time and order of your birth?
How, with a fancy so unkind to mirth,
A sense so hard, a style so worn and bare,
Look ye for any welcome anywhere
From any shelf or heart-home on the earth?

Should others ask you this, say then I yearn'd
To write you such as once, when I was young,
Finding I should have loved and thereto turn'd.
'Twere something yet to live again among
The gentle youth beloved, and where I learn'd
My art, be there remember'd for my song.

LII

Who takes the census of the living dead,
Ere the day come when memory shall o'ercrowd
The kingdom of their fame, and for that proud
And airy people find no room nor stead?
Ere hoarding Time, that ever thrusteth back
The fairest treasures of his ancient store,
Better with best confound, so he may pack
His greedy gatherings closer, more and more?

Let the true Muse rewrite her sullied page,
And purge her story of the men of hate,

That they go dirgeless down to Satan's rage
With all else foul, deform'd and miscreate:
She hath full toil to keep the names of love
Honour'd on earth, as they are bright above.

LIII

I heard great Hector sounding war's alarms,
Where thro' the listless ghosts chiding he strode,
As tho' the Greeks besieged his last abode,
And he his Troy's hope still, her king-at-arms.
But on those gentle meads, which Lethe charms
With weary oblivion, his passion glow'd
Like the cold night-worm's candle, and only show'd
Such mimic flame as neither heats nor harms.

'Twas plain to read, even by those shadows quaint,
How rude catastrophe had dim'd his day,
And blighted all his cheer with stern complaint:
To arms! to arms! what more the voice would say
Was swallow'd in the valleys, and grew faint
Upon the thin air, as he pass'd away.

LIV

Since not the enamour'd sun with glance more fond
Kisses the foliage of his sacred tree,
Than doth my waking thought arise on thee,
Loving none near thee, like thee nor beyond;
Nay, since I am sworn thy slave, and in the bond
Is writ my promise of eternity;
Since to such high hope thou'st encouraged me,
That if thou look but from me I despond;

Since thou'rt my all in all, O think of this:
Think of the dedication of my youth:
Think of my loyalty, my joy, my bliss:
Think of my sorrow, my despair and ruth,
My sheer annihilation if I miss:
Think—if thou shouldst be false—think of thy truth.

LV

These meagre rhymes, which a returning mood
Sometimes o'errateth, I as oft despise;

And knowing them illnatured, stiff and rude,
See them as others with contemptuous eyes.
Nay, and I wonder less at God's respect
For man, a minim jot in time and space,
Than at the soaring faith of His elect,
That gift of gifts, the comfort of His grace.

O truth unsearchable, O heavenly love,
Most infinitely tender, so to touch
The work that we can meanly reckon of:
Surely—I say—we are favour'd overmuch.
But of this wonder, what doth most amaze
Is that we know our love is held for praise.

LVI

Beauty sat with me all the summer day,
Awaiting the sure triumph of her eye;
Nor mark'd I till we parted, how, hard by,
Love in her train stood ready for his prey.
She, as too proud to join herself the fray,
Trusting too much to her divine ally,
When she saw victory tarry, chid him—'Why
Dost thou not at one stroke this rebel slay?'

Then generous Love, who holds my heart in fee,
Told of our ancient truce: so from the fight
We straight withdrew our forces, all the three.
Baffled but not disheartN'd she took flight
Scheming new tactics: Love came home with me,
And prompts my measured verses as I write.

LVII

In autumn moonlight, when the white air wan
Is fragrant in the wake of summer hence,
'Tis sweet to sit entranced, and muse thereon
In melancholy and godlike indolence:
When the proud spirit, lull'd by mortal prime
To fond pretence of immortality,
Vieweth all moments from the birth of time,
All things whate'er have been or yet shall be.

And like the garden, where the year is spent,
The ruin of old life is full of yearning,
Mingling poetic rapture of lament

With flowers and sunshine of spring's sure returning;
Only in visions of the white air wan
By godlike fancy seized and dwelt upon.

LVIII

When first I saw thee, dearest, if I say
The spells that conjure back the hour and place,
And evermore I look upon thy face,
As in the spring of years long pass'd away;
No fading of thy beauty's rich array,
No detriment of age on thee I trace,
But time's defeat written in spoils of grace,
From rivals robb'd, whom thou didst pity and slay.

So hath thy growth been, thus thy faith is true,
Unchanged in change, still to my growing sense,
To life's desire the same, and nothing new:
But as thou wert in dream and prescience
At love's arising, now thou stand'st to view
In the broad noon of his magnificence.

LIX

'Twas on the very day winter took leave
Of those fair fields I love, when to the skies
The fragrant Earth was smiling in surprise
At that her heaven-descended, quick reprieve,
I wander'd forth my sorrow to relieve;
Yet walk'd amid sweet pleasure in such wise
As Adam went alone in Paradise,
Before God of His pity fashion'd Eve.

And out of tune with all the joy around
I laid me down beneath a flowering tree,
And o'er my senses crept a sleep profound;
In which it seem'd that thou wert given to me,
Rending my body, where with hurried sound
I feel my heart beat, when I think of thee.

LX

Love that I know, love I am wise in, love,
My strength, my pride, my grace, my skill untaught,
My faith here upon earth, my hope above,

My contemplation and perpetual thought:
The pleasure of my fancy, my heart's fire,
My joy, my peace, my praise, my happy theme,
The aim of all my doing, my desire
Of being, my life by day, by night my dream:

Love, my sweet melancholy, my distress,
My pain, my doubt, my trouble, my despair,
My only folly and unhappiness,
And in my careless moments still my care:
O love, sweet love, earthly love, love divine,
Say'st thou to-day, O love, that thou art mine?

LXI

The dark and serious angel, who so long
Vex'd his immortal strength in charge of me,
Hath smiled for joy and fled in liberty
To take his pastime with the peerless throng.
Oft had I done his noble keeping wrong,
Wounding his heart to wonder what might be
God's purpose in a soul of such degree;
And there he had left me but for mandate strong.

But seeing thee with me now, his task at close
He knoweth, and wherefore he was bid to stay,
And work confusion of so many foes:
The thanks that he doth look for, here I pay,
Yet fear some heavenly envy, as he goes
Unto what great reward I cannot say.

LXII

I will be what God made me, nor protest
Against the bent of genius in my time,
That science of my friends robs all the best,
While I love beauty, and was born to rhyme.
Be they our mighty men, and let me dwell
In shadow among the mighty shades of old,
With love's forsaken palace for my cell;
Whence I look forth and all the world behold,

And say, These better days, in best things worse,
This bastardy of time's magnificence,
Will mend in fashion and throw off the curse,
To crown new love with higher excellence.

Curs'd tho' I be to live my life alone,
My toil is for man's joy, his joy my own.

LXIII

I live on hope and that I think do all
Who come into this world, and since I see
Myself in swim with such good company,
I take my comfort whatsoe'er befall.
I abide and abide, as if more stout and tall
My spirit would grow by waiting like a tree;
And, clear of others' toil, it pleaseth me
In dreams their quick ambition to forestall.

And if thro' careless eagerness I slide
To some accomplishment, I give my voice
Still to desire, and in desire abide.
I have no stake abroad; if I rejoice
In what is done or doing, I confide
Neither to friend nor foe my secret choice.

LXIV

Ye blessed saints, that now in heaven enjoy
The purchase of those tears, the world's disdain,
Doth Love still with his war your peace annoy,
Or hath Death freed you from his ancient pain?
Have ye no springtide, and no burst of May
In flowers and leafy trees, when solemn night
Pants with love-music, and the holy day
Breaks on the ear with songs of heavenly light?

What make ye and what strive for? keep ye thought
Of us, or in new excellence divine
Is old forgot? or do ye count for nought
What the Greek did and what the Florentine?
We keep your memories well: O in your store
Live not our best joys treasured evermore?

LXV

Ah heavenly joy! But who hath ever heard,
Who hath seen joy, or who shall ever find
Joy's language? There is neither speech nor word;
Nought but itself to teach it to mankind.

Scarce in our twenty thousand painful days
We may touch something: but there lives—beyond
The best of art, or nature's kindest phase—
The hope whereof our spirit is fain and fond:

The cause of beauty given to man's desires
Writ in the expectancy of starry skies,
The faith which gloweth in our fleeting fires,
The aim of all the good that here we prize;
Which but to love, pursue and pray for well
Maketh earth heaven, and to forget it, hell.

LXVI

My wearied heart, whenever, after all,
Its loves and yearnings shall be told complete,
When gentle death shall bid it cease to beat,
And from all dear illusions disenthrall:
However then thou shalt appear to call
My fearful heart, since down at others' feet
It bade me kneel so oft, I'll not retreat
From thee, nor fear before thy feet to fall.

And I shall say, 'Receive this loving heart
Which err'd in sorrow only; and in sin
Took no delight; but being forced apart
From thee, without thee hoping thee to win,
Most prized what most thou madest as thou art
On earth, till heaven were open to enter in.'

LXVII

Dreary was winter, wet with changeful sting
Of clinging snowfall and fast-flying frost;
And bitterer northwinds then withheld the spring,
That dallied with her promise till 'twas lost.
A sunless and half-hearted summer drown'd
The flowers in needful and unwelcom'd rain;
And Autumn with a sad smile fled uncrown'd
From fruitless orchards and unripen'd grain.

But coud the skies of this most desolate year
In its last month learn with our love to glow,
Men yet should rank its cloudless atmosphere
Above the sunsets of five years ago:
Of my great praise too part should be its own,

Now reckon'd peerless for thy love alone.

LXVIII

Away now, lovely Muse, roam and be free:
Our commerce ends for aye, thy task is done:
Tho' to win thee I left all else unwon,
Thou, whom I most have won, art not for me.
My first desire, thou too forgone must be,
Thou too, O much lamented now, tho' none
Will turn to pity thy forsaken son,
Nor thy divine sisters will weep for thee.

None will weep for thee: thou return, O Muse,
To thy Sicilian fields: I once have been
On thy loved hills, and where thou first didst use
Thy sweetly balanced rhyme, O thankless queen,
Have pluck'd and wreath'd thy flowers; but do thou choose
Some happier brow to wear thy garlands green.

LXIX

Eternal Father, who didst all create,
In whom we live, and to whose bosom move,
To all men be Thy name known, which is Love,
Till its loud praises sound at heaven's high gate.
Perfect Thy kingdom in our passing state,
That here on earth Thou may'st as well approve
Our service, as Thou ownest theirs above,
Whose joy we echo and in pain await.

Grant body and soul each day their daily bread:
And should in spite of grace fresh woe begin,
Even as our anger soon is past and dead
Be Thy remembrance mortal of our sin:
By Thee in paths of peace Thy sheep be led,
And in the vale of terror comforted.

Robert Seymour Bridges – A Short Biography

Robert Seymour Bridges, OM was born on 23 October 1844 at Walmer in Kent where he spent his early childhood in a house overlooking the anchoring ground of the British fleet. He was the fourth son and eighth child of John Thomas Bridges (1805–1853) and Harriett Elizabeth Affleck (1807–1897).

His father died at the age of only 47 in 1853 and a year later his mother remarried and the family relocated to Rochdale, where his stepfather, John Edward Nassau Molesworth, was the vicar.

In 1854 Bridges was sent to the elite public school of Eton College and attended there until 1863. Whilst there he met the poet Digby Mackworth Dolben and Lionel Muirhead, who became a lifelong friend.

After Eton he went to Oxford and the Corpus Christi College. Whilst studying he became good friends with Gerald Manley Hopkins. Hopkins is now considered the superior poet and Bridges probably knew this or at least was a great admirer as he was essential in ensuring the publication of the complete works of Hopkins in 1918. His edition of Hopkins's poems is considered a major contribution to English literature.

He received his degree and graduated from Oxford in 1867 with a second class in literae humaniores. His initial thought was to enter religious life with the Church of England and he travelled to the Middle East in furtherance of his knowledge on the subject. But instead he decided that life as a physician would be a better path and after learning German for eight months in Germany (that being the language of many scientific papers at the time) he began his study of medicine at St. Bartholomew's Hospital in 1869. His long term hope was that by the age of forty he could retire from medicine to devote himself to writing.

Bridges failed his final medical examinations in 1873 and as unable to immediately retake the papers, spent six months in Italy learning Italian and as much as he could about Italian art. In July 1874 he went to study medicine in Dublin. Re-examined in December of that year, he obtained his MB and became a house physician to Dr Patrick Black at St Bartholomew's Hospital.

He practiced as a casualty physician at this teaching hospital where he also engaged in a series of highly critical remarks about the Victorian medical establishment. Such was his workload that he claimed that whilst working as a young doctor he saw a staggering 30,940 patients in one year.

After being a house physician at St Bartholomew's he later became casualty physician and later assistant physician at the Hospital for Sick Children, Great Ormond Street, and then physician at Great Northern Hospital, Holloway.

A bout of severe pneumonia and lung disease forced his retirement from the medical profession in 1882 and so slightly ahead of schedule he began his literary career in earnest.

However he had, prior to this, been writing for several years. His first collection of poems having been published in 1873. Indeed its worth pointing out that his early materials were published privately, mainly to be given away to friends and his small circle of admirers as they sold little. It took Bridges some time to gain traction and a wider audience.

After his illness and a trip to Italy with Muirhead, Bridges moved with his mother to Yattendon in Berkshire.

It was during his residence in Yattendon, from 1882 to 1904, that Bridges wrote most of his best-known lyrics as well as eight plays and two masques, all in verse.

It was here that he first met and then in 1884 he married Monica Waterhouse, daughter of Alfred Waterhouse R.A., the famous architect. The couple had three children: Elizabeth (1887–1977), Margaret (1889–1926), and Edward Ettingdene Bridges (1892–1969). They would spend the rest of their lives in rural seclusion, in an idyllic marriage, first at Yattendon, Berkshire, then later at Boars Hill, Oxford

Bridges made an important contribution to hymnody with the publication in 1899 of his Yattendon Hymnal, which he created specifically for musical reasons. This collection of hymns, although not a financial success, became a bridge between the Victorian hymnody of the last half of the 19th century and the modern hymnody of the early 20th century. He was a chorister at Yattendon church for 18 years.

In 1902 Monica and his daughter Margaret became seriously ill with tuberculosis, and a move from Yattendon to a healthier climate was in order.

After living in several temporary homes they moved abroad to spend a year in Switzerland, and finally returning settled again in England at Chilswell House, which Bridges had designed and which was built on Boar's Hill overlooking Oxford University.

Bridges was elected to the Fellowship of the Royal College of Physicians of London in 1900.

His greatest achievement though was still some years ahead of him. The office of Poet Laureate was held by Alfred Austin but with his death it was offered first to Rudyard Kipling, who refused it, and thence to Bridges. He was appointed Poet Laureate in 1913 by George V, the only medical graduate to have ever held the office. It seems a strange choice given the 'write to order' brief of Poet Laureate but Bridges accepted and must have known of the strictures.

That same year along with Henry Bradley and Walter Raleigh he founded the Society for Pure English.

Bridges received advice from the young phonetician David Abercrombie on the reformed spelling system he was devising for the publication of his collected essays (later published in seven volumes by Oxford University Press, with the help of the distinguished typographer Stanley Morison, who designed the new letters). Thus Robert Bridges contributed to phonetics.

The office of Poet Laureate has been held by many great and well known poets such as John Dryden, William Wordsworth and Alfred Lord Tennyson.

Bridges at this stage was not highly regarded nor well known but more a safe pair of hands in a World rapidly being overshadowed by the storms about to erupt over Europe and the First World War.

The events of the First World War, including the wounding of his son, Edward, had a sobering effect on Bridges' poetry. He composed fiercely patriotic poems and letters, and in 1915 edited a volume of prose and poetry, The Spirit of Man, intended to appeal to readers living in war times.

One area where his work did resonate though was with a great many composers and specifically British. Many set his poetry to music and among them were Hubert Parry, Gustav Holst and Gerald Finzi.

Despite being made poet laureate Bridges was never a very well-known poet and only achieved his great popularity shortly before his death with The Testament of Beauty.

His best-known poems are found in the two earlier volumes of Shorter Poems (1890, 1894). His talents did not stop at poetry and his works include verse plays and literary criticism, including a study of the work of fellow poet John Keats.

As a poet Bridges stands rather apart from the tide of modern English verse, but his work has had great influence in a select circle, by its restraint, purity, precision, and delicacy yet strength of expression. It embodies a distinct theory of prosody. Bridges' deep faith underpinned much of his work.

In the book Milton's Prosody, he took an empirical approach to examining Milton's use of blank verse, and developed the somewhat controversial theory that Milton's practice was essentially syllabic. He considered free verse to be too limiting, and explained his position in the essay "Humdrum and Harum-Scarum".

Bridge's own efforts to "free" verse resulted in the poems he called "Neo-Miltonic Syllabics", which were collected in New Verse (1925). The metre of these poems was based on syllables rather than accents, and he used the principle again in the long philosophical poem The Testament of Beauty (1929), for which he received the Order of Merit. Perhaps The Testament of Beauty is his most highly regarded work but he also wrote and also translated historic hymns, and many of these were included in Songs of Syon (1904) and the later English Hymnal (1906). Several of Bridges' hymns and translations are still in use today.

Bridges work with the Society for Pure English (S.P.E.) was interrupted by the War but resumed in 1919. The work for the S.P.E. led to Bridges' only trip to America in 1924, during which he increased interest in the group among American scholars.

As previously mentioned his masterpiece, a long philosophical poem entitled The Testament of Beauty, was begun on Christmas Day, 1924, with fourteen lines of what he referred to as "loose Alexandrines." He set the piece aside until 1926, when the death of his daughter Margaret prompted him to resume work as a way to ease his grief. The Testament of Beauty was published in October 1929, one day after his eighty-fifth birthday and six months before his death.

A Victorian who by choice remained apart from the aesthetic movements of his day, Robert Bridges was a classicist and experimented with eighteenth-century classical forms..

On December 2nd 1929 he was pictured on the cover that week of Time Magazine

Robert Seymour Bridges' health was failing and undermined by cancer and its complications he died at his home, Chilswell, on 21 April 1930. His ashes are buried near the family cross in the churchyard of St Peter and St Paul's Church, Yattendon, Berkshire.

The cross was originally erected by Bridges in memory of his mother Harriet Elizabeth. There is also a memorial tablet to him inside the church.

Robert Seymour Bridges – A Concise Bibliography

Poetry collections
The Growth of Love (1876; 1889; 1898), a sequence of (24; 79; 69) sonnets
Prometheus the Firegiver: A Mask in the Greek Manner (1883)
Eros and Psyche: A Narrative Poem in Twelve Measures (1885; 1894), a story from the Latin of Apuleius
Shorter Poems, Books I–IV (1890)
Shorter Poems, Books I–V (1894)
New Poems (1899)
Demeter: A Mask (1905), performed 1904
Ibant Obscuri: An Experiment in the Classical Hexameter (1916), with reprint of summary of Stone's Prosody, accompanied by 'later observations & modifications'
October and Other Poems (1920)
The Tapestry: Poems (1925), in neo-Miltonic syllabics
New Verse (1926),
The Testament of Beauty (1929)

Verse drama
Nero (1885), historical tragedy; called The First Part of Nero after the publication of Nero: Part II
The Feast of Bacchus (1889); partly translated from the Heauton-Timoroumenos of Terence
Achilles in Scyros (1890), a drama in a mixed manner
Palicio (1890), a romantic drama in five acts in the Elizabethan manner
The Return of Ulysses (1890), a drama in five acts in a mixed manner
The Christian Captives (1890), a tragedy in five acts in a mixed manner; on the same subject as Calderón's El Principe Constante
The Humours of the Court (1893), a comedy in three acts; founded on Calderón's El secreto á voces and on Lope de Vega's El Perro del hortelano
Nero, Part II (1894)

Prose
Milton's Prosody, With a Chapter on Accentual Verse (1893; 1901; 1921), based on essays published in 1887 and 1889
Keats (1895)
Hymns from the Yattendon Hymnal (1899)
The Spirit of Man (1916)
Poems of Gerard Manley Hopkins (1918), edited with notes by R.B.
The Necessity of Poetry (1918)
Collected Essays, Papers, Etc. (1927–36)

www.ingramcontent.com/pod-product-compliance
Lightning Source LLC
Chambersburg PA
CBHW060105050426
42448CB00011B/2630